Amazing life cycles

MAMMALS

John Allan

Female Warthogs who have lost their litter often act as foster mothers for other piglets.

Contents

Words that look **bold like this** are in the glossary.

ISBN 978 1 912108 114

First published in Great Britain in 2019 by
Hungry Tomato Ltd, The Old Bakery Studios, Blewetts Wharf,
Malpas Road, Truro, Cornwall, TR1 1QH, UK

Manufactured in the United States of America

What is a mammal?

Discover how mammals live from their first days to when they grow old. Look at some amazing mammals and their life cycles.

A Mammals is . . .

. . . an animal that is warm blooded. This means their body **temperature** stays about the same, no matter how hot or cold the air or water is around them.

Mammals also have hair on their bodies. An elephant is a mammal with smooth skin covered in tiny hairs. It also has hair in its ears and on its nose.

Most mammals give birth to live babies. When a mammal baby is born, the mother feeds it with milk from inside her body. This is called suckling.

Did you know that people are mammals too?

Mammals can be tiny like a mouse lemur or enormous like an elephant!

AMAZING MAMMAL FACT

Bats are the only mammals that can fly.

Mammal habitats

AMAZING MAMMAL FACT
Many African grassland mammals, such as lions, sleep during the day and hunt at night when it is cool.

A habitat is the place where a plant or an animal lives. Mammals live in hot desert habitats and cold, icy places, such as the Arctic. Mammals such as whales and seals live in the ocean.

Seals are mammals that can live in the icy, snowy Arctic.

Mammals live in most of the world's habitats.

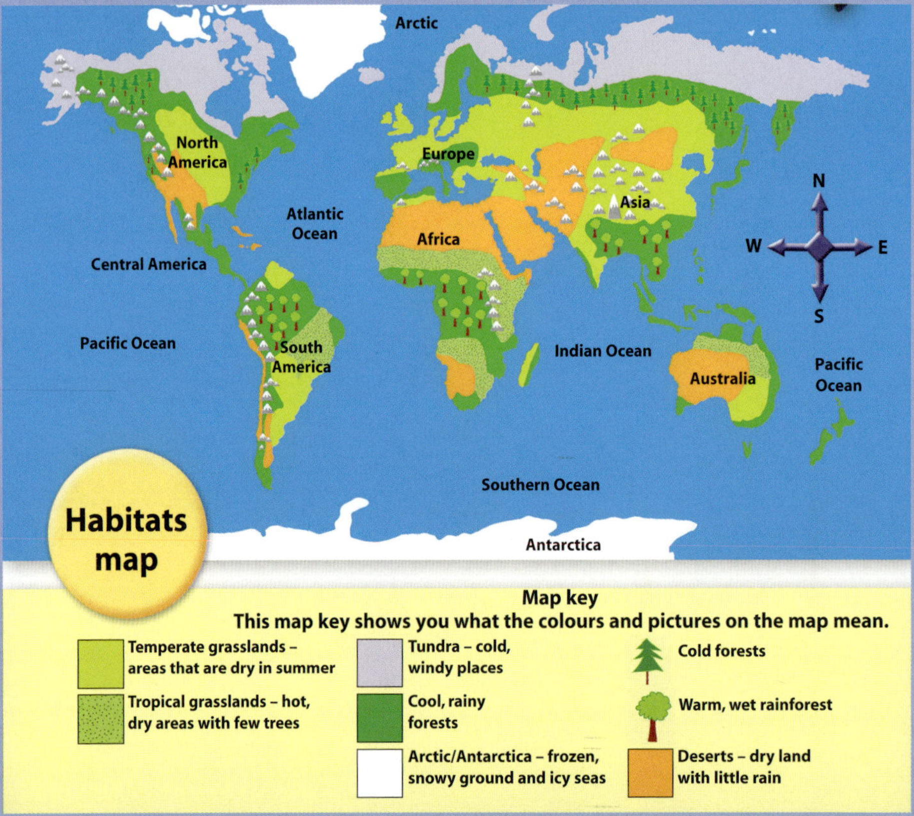

Rainforests are warm, wet habitats with lots of trees and plants. Mammals such as monkeys, gorillas, and sloths live here.

Sloths hang upside down.

Grasslands are hot, dry habitats. Mammals such as rhinos, elephants, lions and meerkats, live in the grasslands in Africa.

Meat-eating mammals

***Animals that eat meat are called* carnivores*. These mammals have sharp claws and teeth to help them catch and eat their* prey*. Animals that hunt are called* predators.**

Big cats such as tigers and cheetahs are carnivores.

AMAZING MAMMAL FACT

Orcas are also called killer whales because they kill and eat seals, penguins, and other whales.

Sometimes orcas surf onto a beach to catch their prey. The waves then pull them back out to sea.

The giant anteater uses its long nose and long, sticky tongue to scoop up bugs

This long-eared bat is hunting a moth.

Bats are nocturnal. This means they sleep during the day and go hunting at night.

Cheetah's have to run very fast to catch their meals!

A cheetah can run up to 74 mph.

Can the springbok run faster than the cheetah and escape?

Plant-eating mammals

Animals that only eat plants are called* herbivores*. They eat leaves, roots, fruit, or flowers. These mammals have developed special ways to help them eat the food they need.

AMAZING MAMMAL FACT

Hippos use their wide lips to grab grass. Then they swing their heads from side to side to pull up the grass from the roots.

Hippos live in Africa. In the day they keep cool in rivers. They come out of the river at sunset to eat grass during the night.

A koala has a home tree where it lives.

Koalas only eat one type of food—the leaves of the eucalyptus tree. These trees grow in Australia where koalas live.

Koalas spend their time eating and sleeping in the eucalyptus trees.

Warthogs use their strong snouts to dig for tasty roots in the hard ground.

Warthogs live on African grasslands.

Mom meets Dad

Grizzly bear males don't help care for their babies and can sometimes eat them.

***Some mammals* mate and then bring up their young together. Other mammals mate and then the female looks after the babies alone or with other females in a group.**

When a male orca is grown-up and ready to mate, he goes to another pod and mates with a female. Then he goes back to live with his mother in his family group. Female orcas bring up their babies in their family group.

Orca couple swims around each other—it's like dancing!

AMAZING MAMMAL FACT

Orcas stay with their mothers all their lives. They live in family groups called pods.

A male and a female meerkat will become a couple. They lead a family group and are the only ones in the group allowed to have babies.

Male warthogs fight over who gets to mate with a female.

After a male and female warthog mate, the male leaves. Adult male warthogs live on their own.

What is a life cycle?

A life cycle is all the different* stages *and changes that an animal or plant goes through in its life. This diagram shows a mammal life cycle.

A baby lion is called a cub.

1 A female mammal gives birth to a live baby or babies.

This is the of a

6 When they become adults, male and female mammals meet and mate.

5 Some mammals live with their family group when they grow up. Some go off and live on their own.

Lions are meat-eaters.

2 Female mammals feed their babies milk.

life cycle lion.

3 Mammal mothers look after their babies. Sometimes the fathers help too.

4 Mammals teach their babies how to hunt, or find food. Young meat-eaters practice their hunting skills on each other.

Bats

Bats usually have one baby each year. Hundreds of female bats gather together to give birth in a cave or a building.

A baby bat is called a pup. When the pups are born, the mothers and pups stay together in a huge group called a nursery roost.

At 10-14 weeks, pups can fly by themselves, between trees and their camp.

A mother bat can find her own pup among hundreds of other bats. She knows its smell and its sound.

A newborn pup will cling to its mother's fur, if she needs' to carry it to another place.

This pup is suckling from its mother.

LIFE CYCLE FACTS

A flying fox bat usualy has just one baby a year. She will carry the baby for about five months.

AMAZING MAMMAL LIFE CYCLE

Giant anteaters

Giant anteaters live in hot, dry grasslands in South America. Anteaters live alone. They only come together to mate.

This anteater uses its tongue to scoop up some bugs from inside a fallen tree.

The female giant anteater gives birth standing on her back legs.

After a few months, the baby hops off its mother's back to explore and then hops on again.

The baby stays with its mother until it is about two years old.

LIFE CYCLE FACTS

Giant anteaters are pregnant for 190 days. Females start to have babies when they are about 3 years old.

If the baby falls off, it grunts to let mom know.

AMAZING MAMMAL FACT

The baby anteater is born with fur and sharp claws. It crawls onto its mother's back where she licks it clean. Baby anteaters suckle for about six months.

Orcas

Orca babies, called calves, are born underwater tail first. An orca calf can be 7.5 feet (2.4 m) long when it is born!

This calf has come to the surface to look at a whale-watching boat. The boat has visitors on it looking at the whales.

The mother orca teaches the calf how to hunt and catch food.

Orca families talk to each other using grunts, whistles, and squeals. Calves learn how to make these sounds.

As soon as the calf is born, the mother orca uses her flippers and her nose, to guide it to the surface, for its first breath of air.

Most orca pods have about 30 members.

LIFE CYCLE FACTS

Orcas are pregnant for 15 to 18 months. Females start to have babies when they are about 15 years old.

AMAZING MAMMAL LIFE CYCLE

Meerkats

Meerkats live in groups that include males, females, and babies. They live in burrows under the ground.

The dark rings around its eyes protect the meerkat's eyes from the bright sunlight.

LIFE CYCLE FACTS

Meerkats are pregnant for 75 days. A female starts to have babies when she is one year old.

Adult meerkats take turns babysitting while others go hunting.

When they are about one month old, baby meerkats, called kits, start to learn how to hunt. Each kit has an adult that teaches it how to hunt.

Newborn kits are helpless and do not have hair. They are born in the burrow and stay there until they are three to four weeks old.

This mom is suckling her newborn kits. They are 9 days old.

Meerkats stand up on their back legs . . .

. . . to watch for predators such as eagles.

Warthogs

Female warthogs give birth to two or three babies at a time in an underground burrow. The babies, or piglets, leave the burrow when they are about two weeks old.

LIFE CYCLE FACT

Warthogs are pregnant for 6 months. A female starts to have babies when she is 18 months old.

Warthog piglets are not born with tusks. The tusks grow as the baby grows.

It is important that the newborn piglets do not get wet or cold. They sleep on a raised shelf at the back of the burrow to make sure they stay dry.

Warthogs use their sharp **tusks** to fight off predators such as lions. Both male and female warthogs have tusks.

The piglets suckle for about four months. Male piglets stay with their mother for about two years. Females go off on their own when they are about 18 months old.

AMAZING MAMMAL LIFE CYCLE

Hippopotamuses

Hippos live in groups called herds. A herd includes one adult male, lots of females, and their young.

LIFE CYCLE FACT

Hippos are pregnant for 8 months. A female starts to have babies when she is 9 years old.

The hippo baby, or calf, is born in shallow water at the edge of the river. The mother quickly pushes the baby to the surface so it can breathe.

Most adult hippos stay in the herd where they were born. A male hippo may start his own herd when he is about 20 years old.

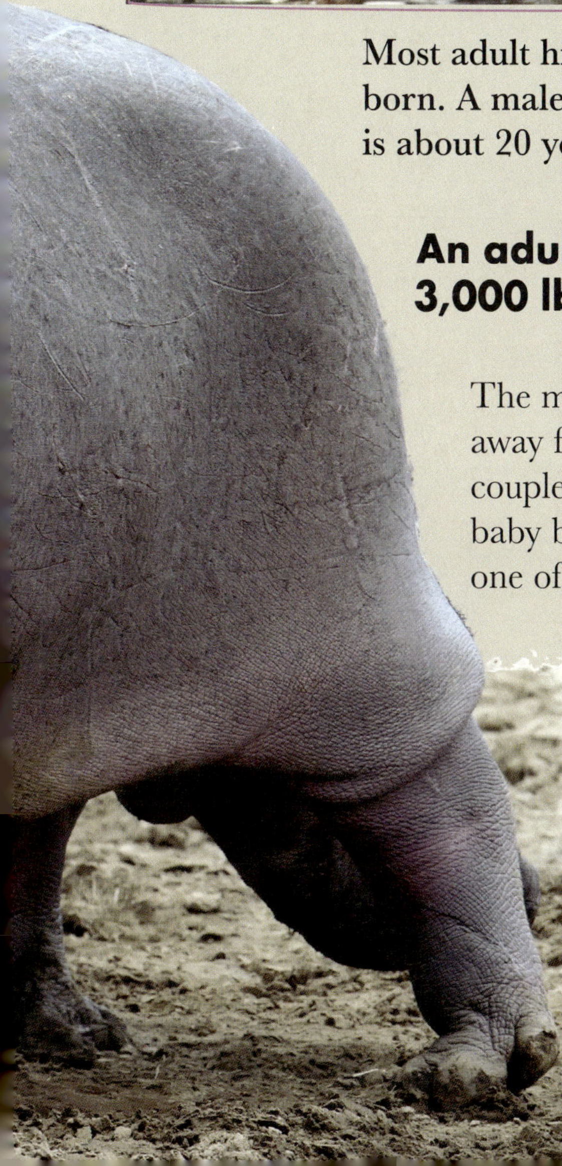

An adult hippo can weigh 3,000 lbs (1.5 tons).

The mother and calf move away from the herd for the first couple of weeks. This stops the baby being accidentally hurt by one of the other adults.

AMAZING MAMMAL FACT

Sometimes a hippo calf will rest on its mother's back. It will slip into the water if it gets too hot and then climb back up.

AMAZING MAMMAL LIFE CYCLE

Koalas

Koalas are marsupials. This means that the mother has a pouch on her tummy where her baby lives. The pouch is a bit like a pocket. A newborn koala is called a joey.

Joey

The newborn joey is tiny! It has no hair, and it can't see or hear. It crawls into its mother's pouch. The joey suckles in the pouch.

The joey's fur, ears and eyes grow. The joey gets bigger and bigger. When the joey is about six to seven months old it starts to ride on its mother's back.

At about one year old, the koala leaves its mother. This is usually when the mother gives birth to another joey.

LIFE CYCLE FACT

Koalas are pregnant for 35 days. A female starts to have babies when she is 2 years old.

That's amazing!

All mammal moms care for their babies. They feed them milk and teach them how to find food. But mammal babies begin life in lots of different ways!

Female polar bears go to sleep in a den for the winter. While they are in the den they give birth to their babies, called cubs.

AMAZING MAMMAL FACT
The newborn polar bear cubs are about 30 centimetres long. They are blind, pink and hairless.

The polar bear's den is under the snow.

A baby giraffe is called a calf.

A newborn giraffe is 1.8 metres tall!

The female platypus lays two or three grape-sized eggs. The eggs **hatch** about 12 days later.

AMAZING MAMMAL FACT

The duck billed platypus is a very, very unusual mammal because it lays eggs!

The giraffe is the world's tallest animal mum. The female gives birth standing up. The giraffe calf drops two metres to the ground!

Glossary

burrows – Tunnels and holes under the ground where some animals live.
carnivores – Animals which eat meat. These animals are also predators.
desert – A place where it hardly ever rains. Deserts can be very hot in the day. Some deserts get cold at night.
hatch – When a baby bird or animal breaks out of its egg. It is like being born.
herbivores – Animals which do not eat meat. Herbivores eat foods such as grass, leaves, fruits and flowers.
mate – When a male and female animal meet and have babies.
predators – Animals which hunt and kill other animals for food.
prey – Animals which are hunted by other animals as food.
scorpion – A Small animal with eight legs, two arms with big claws, and a tail with a poisonous sting.
stages – Different times of an animal's life when the animal changes in some way.
temperature – How hot or cold something is.
tusks – Long, sharp pointed teeth.

Index

Picture credits
Shutterstock. 1: Patryk Kosmider. 2-3: jDross75. 4-5: By jeep 2499, By Foto 4440., Karel Gallas, Martin Janca, Elena Erasmus. 6-7: Eric Iseelee4a, Ian Duffield, Costas anton dumitrescu, Sebastiaan Peeters. 8-9: wildestanima, Leornardo Gonzalez7, Tasha Bubo, Uwe Bergwitz, Daria Rybakova., 10-11: Dave Pusey, Anthony Carneiro, Stuart G Porter, Sergey Uryadnikov, Teresa Moore, Art Media Factory, Eric Isselee, Orthgon. 12-13: Ivan Kuzman, Benjamin B, Nate Samui, Kajornyot wildlife photorgraphy, Hendrasu. 14-15: GR92100, Pascale Gueret. 16-17: Chase Dekker, widestanima, Tory Kallman, Christian Musat, TOSP. 16-17: Susan Flashman, Svetlana Foote, Mrinal Pat, Sergraff, Kelsey Green, EcoPrint. 18-19: Rudi Hulshof, Fred Turk, Clickit, Dawie Jacobs Photography, Iakov Filiminov. 20-21: Stuart G Porter, Stephen Raats, Stefano Cavanna, Volodymyr Burdiak, Dennis Jacobsen. 22-23: By Covenenant, Andrew Burteleit, worlds wildlife wonders, Alizada Studios, Apple2499. 24-25: Jen Watson, John Carnemolla, Belovodchenko, Sergey Uryadnikov, Andre Anita, Dave Pussey